T0207705

A Spiritual Walk With God

Testimonials And Sermons

CYNTHIA PRIEST HUFF

WESTBOW
PRESS®
A DIVISION OF THOMAS NELSON
& ZONDERVAN

This book is a work of non-fiction. Unless otherwise noted, the author and the publisher make no explicit guarantees as to the accuracy of the information contained in this book and in some cases, names of people and places have been altered to protect their privacy.

WestBow Press books may be ordered through booksellers or by contacting:

WestBow Press
A Division of Thomas Nelson & Zondervan
1663 Liberty Drive
Bloomington, IN 47403
www.westbowpress.com
844-714-3454

Scripture taken from the King James Version of the Bible.

ISBN: 978-1-6642-5266-0 (sc)
ISBN: 978-1-6642-5265-3 (hc)
ISBN: 978-1-6642-5264-6 (e)

Library of Congress Control Number: 2021924829

Print information available on the last page.

WestBow Press rev. date: 12/20/2021

Contents

Dedication ix

Vision 1
Morning Prayer 2
My story... 3
Basic training.. 8
My Testimony 10
Birth Of El- Shaddai 12
God Delivers a Miracle 14
Encounter with God... 16
What Wives Need to Know..................................... 18
God has a Purpose for You...................................... 19
Seeing through the eyes of God.............................. 22
What makes you Live.. 25
Learning how to win in your life............................ 27
The Call 29
The Eyes of God.. 31
Arms of God 34
The Biggest Lesson 35
This is what life will teach you 36
What your complaint's actually reveal about your heart....... 37
life is a wonder 39

God's Clouds..40

What is Radical faith 43

Trials of life..44

Trusting the winds of God......................................48

Life is like a breath of air 50

Having the peace in your life 52

God's Unconditional Love.......................................54

You are God's Daughter...56

Man and Woman of God 57

God's timing 60

The Season of life..61

The Strategies of Jesus..62

Why does God collect our tears in a bottle 63

Tears a Language God-understands 65

God's Purpose...67

Be careful of your Thoughts 69

People are watching you..71

God's Strength 73

God's Love 74

Aging in God 75

God's Sovereign Love..77

The Breath of God...79

In the palm of God's hand 80

Through the storm...84

Understanding the seasons of life 86

Growing Gracefully 88

How to age Gracefully 89

Over Coming Doubts...90

Awesome God 91

People Change...92

The angel from above 93

Faith in Action..94

We must Remove Our Mask 95
Do you have a Goliath in your life 97
Giving trust in God's Provision 99
Your Child 100
Conclusion 101
My Lover My Savior 103
Greatest Gift 104
Let me rest in you 105
My wonderful wife 106
Jesus Valentine's Day 107
God's Love 108
Facing Struggles 109

Dedication

I consider myself highly blessed to have been led by the Holy Spirit into the call of a Prophetess. It has been a wonderful journey with my Lord and Savior. There were two people in my life, they were my Mother June, and my Grandmother Pearl who were prayer warriors. They would pray for me daily that God would use me in a mighty way one day in the kingdom of God. My mother and grandma taught me how to pray, and how to see people through the eyes of God. I thank God for giving me such a wonderful mother, and grandma that has the love, mercy, and Grace of God within them. My mother and a grandma believe that God would answer their prayers for my life. I have also been blessed by some wonderful people that God sent into my life. Kathy Crag, Asona.

Prophetess Sue Ellen Pastor Shook
Isaac, Kara, Axel
Mandy, Isaiah
Apostle James

Prophetess Velta Gilbert, Ella Coleman Carroll, Apostle Earnest, and Medina and Prophetess Carmelita Nkrumah, Curtis Ward. My Mother June and my Husband Mark who inspired and Keetsie my daughter who encourages me to write all my sermons Stories in my book, and gets it to publish, so others can be blessed in their lives and be encouraged.

The purpose of this book is to help inmates who are incarcerated, desire a new lease on life and how to live a productive life in society. This book can help with depression and hopefully be used as a method for preventing suicide. Last but not least this will help fund my treatments for my lymphedema. Lymphedema has no cure. Your help and contribution to help my endeavor is appreciated more that you will ever know.

I want to thank God for the experience of my first book by stretching me and helping me to grow in many ways of my life and showing me how to look at each situation in my life.

Vision

God gave me a vision when I was 10 years old, which would impact my life. The scriptural basis is

Sometimes we need to pray for the understanding of a vision or an interpretation. When I was eighteen years old, the Lord gave me a vision of the Ministry I would be in. Look at Ezekiel 1:27-28

God does speak in dreams and visions, and in the middle of the night, when people are in a deep sleep head lying on their beds. Joel 2:28 and Job 33:14-15. God gave me a vision when I was 10 years old, which would impact my life. The scriptural basis is Habakkuk 2:2-4 which says one God gives a vision; he wants to see it through until it comes to pass. God reveals himself to us through vision and dreams that will come to pass in the future. Sometimes we need to pray for

The need to pray for the understanding of a vision or an interpretation. When I was eighteen years old, the Lord gave me a vision of the Ministry. I would be in God does speak in dreams and visions, and in the middle of the night, when God does speak in dreams, and visions, and in the middle of the night When people are in a deep sleep head laying on their bed.

Morning Prayer

Father God, I Come to you as your child, asking for you to fill this child up completely with your anointing oil "to pour upon your child; from the top of her head to every part of her body, so as this child goes along her way today., let my life send the glow of your glory. Father let thy oil that is all around me heal, every heart, bondage in people's lives. Father just one touch from your oil, and wine will bring healing to the divine two every wounded soul. Let it flow and set your people free. Let the bondage, and chains drop to the ground setting them free. As your child lord walking on the path that you have put this child on; let this child's life shine for the glory of God. Thank you, Father, for your mercy and Grace you have placed on my life. Thank you for showing me the way out, and for setting me free.

My story

My mother lived with her mother with 5 kids. My mom was divorced and at that time I was just a baby in my mother's arms. Years went by, and now Am 4 years old. My mother was seeing a man. The following week my mother brought him by to meet us. My mother told him if she married him, he must love her children as if they were his very own, so Ronald said yes. He looked at all 5 of us and said may I be your father? All five of us hugged him and he said I love you all. I spoke up and said what is a father? He just laughs with a smile on his face. The next day we all went to school. My brother Dennis was so excited and told everyone in the class and yelled out loud I have a father. In 1957 I started first grade and had a great Teacher. When I got into third grade, I had a harder time with my work. One day Miss Bullying, my teacher said she wanted to give me a test to see how she could help me. Miss Bulling corrected my test papers that showed that I needed help, so she talked to my parents and the decision to place me in a classroom for children with special needs.

When the children at school found out that I was put in a special Ed class. The next day when I entered the bus and I sat down the children would mistreat me by pulling my hair, and say I was a nobody because I was in special Ed. I would begin to cry and when I would get on the bus the children could make fun of me and pull my hair on the bus. There were times my brother Dennis would pull the kids off me from beating me up. Every day when I would get off the bus, the kids would sometimes spit in my face, and say that I was a nobody and that I would be better off dead. This would occur frequently on and off the bus. As I would walk home some of the kids would degrade me; and they would hold me so that they could slug me in the stomach. They would throw stones and laugh at me. The children would mock and call me names, make fun of being developmentally challenged or of my stutter. This would continue till one day a precious Godly woman, that lived on the Conner near the bus stop.

Alice stood on her porch one day and told the children that they were doing wrong and that every human began to be a person. Alice would ask me to sit with her on the porch and have some milk and cookies with her. As I was eating, Alice was telling me how important I was in the eyes of God; that God has a special plan for my life. Alice began to tell me that she was going to take me halfway home from school. When I got home, I would just cry and say am I what these kids say I am.

The pain I felt was so deep, that I would go into my make-believe world, where I felt safe. I would go into my mother's room and lock the door and, look in the big minor I would visualize speaking in front of a big church, before many people whose lives would be touched by the songs of God in my heart. I would visualize being on TV. When I was around my family, they would have to listen to understand what I was saying, because I stuttered badly. On my 10th birthday, I remember this was an extremely exciting day because we were going to see my grandma, Nylund. My grandma Pearl was a Minister and was a prayer warrior. My mother and grandma would pray daily for a miracle to take place in my life. In my home, sitting in the back seat, I was crying very quietly. I looked out the window because it was a beautiful starry night. I said, is there a God, who could love a person like me, and is there any hope for a nobody like me. The tears began to run down my cheeks, and a presence that I have never felt before came upon me.

I heard a still small voice saying to me, looking out through the window, and as I looked out, I rubbed my eyes and said to myself, am really seeing what I think I am seeing. Jesus standing on the right hand of the father, and I saw people and angels behind the people and a big rainbow behind them. I rub my eyes again and lookup. There was an image that looked like a picture of Jesus in the bible. Jesus was on a chariot of white horses coming down to earth with many people on white horses following him, and his angel. Then as it was coming towards me the chariot of white horses vanished away. I then felt a presence coming upon me, that was so peaceful, and I felt safe. At that time, I did not know that it was the Holy Spirit. I heard a voice saying to me, be still my little one, not cry; I am the Lord thy God, who is during you. so, peace Am going to heal you and raise you up, for my glory and my kingdom, and I have called you as my Minster to my people, to raise the dead, heal the broken heart, and set my people free, and in those days, I will bring a godly man and woman who will truly be your friend, and believe your vision that I have given you. For I have called you into the minster, and you will see these things come to pass in the future, so the child is still and knows that I have spoken to you this night forth. I shall call you, my sunshine1969.

Years later God sent me a Christian friend in my life. Her name was Judy. One day during the month of May. Judy called me and asked me if I would go with her and her mother to

Faholo Park in Grass Lake, Michigan, where they were having camp meetings. We are going out to the church campgrounds to help clean up the grounds for 3 days. I asked my mother if I could go with Judy at first, but then she gave it some thought and said that I could go with her mother to the campgrounds. After we had attended the campgrounds, we began walking to pick up trash; and cleaning up the inside of the building to get ready for evening worship. My friend Judy Introduced me to the caretakers (Pastor)daughter, she was fourteen years old.

While we were walking around picking up trash the Holy Spirit said look up, to our left what do you see! I see a young man who looks around 18 that is coming my way. I then heard a still small voice saying to me; Behold your husband the one I have chosen for you. Do not say anything in the way I have told you for Mark will run away. I said to the Lord! This man will not like me the way I am because I stutter, but the Lord said to be still and know I am doing the work. Finally, the service started. Before I sat down, we ran into Mark (my future husband) and I asked him to sit with us, and said I guess I could. The service began as you could hear the music being playing songs from the hymn book. We sat down, and the Evangelist Jimmy Swaggart began to minister the word of healing through the blood of Jesus. Then he prayed. He asked the people who needed special healing to come forward and receive your healing. The Holy Spirit prompted me in my heart to go down and I asked Mark if he would go down with me. Mark said I think I'll just stay here while you go down, but the Holy Spirit was tugging on his heart and for some reason; Mark went down with me to get my healing and saw the miracle before his eyes unfold. God gave back what the enemy stole in my life. God does it all the way. Since that day Mark and I have been going out for 6 months One evening when he came over to take me out that evening, he got on one knee and looked at me and said Cynthia with every beat of my heart will you be my wife and live with me forever I said Yes.

Basic training

In 1970 Mark went in the Air Force basic training at Lack-land AFB for 6 weeks, then sent to Okinawa Japan. We married 6 months later, when I joined him there. Sense than we have been to station Michigan, Florida, and Hickman A.F.B Hawaii I had a friend that had a Christian TV show called me up and said the Hostess that was supposed to come got sick so could you take her place. Yes, I would love to. This was a dream come true. What an exciting moment in my life. Everything this world said I would not be able to do, God brought it to pass in my life. My husband retired with 21 1\2 years in 1992.Mark got a phone call and asked if he would like a job in Columbus Ohio working at DFAS working with the government. In January 2021 Mark will have 11 years working there.

In 2011 her daughter passed away at the age 39 years old. I took care of her for 1 year. One day I went into her room, my daughter Keetsie looked at me and said mommy Jesus said to me in 3 days I will get you and take you home in my chariot into heaven. Mommy the Holy Spirit said that he is going to give you your beautiful home for the minister, I said thank you Jesus. I prayed over Keetsie and told Keetsie that I loved Her so much. We were not just mom and daughter, we were friends. Keetsie was my only daughter. The third day came, God took keetsie home just as she said. That morning around 9 am. I walked into her room, and I knew she was in heaven. I touched her keetsie was still warm than I screamed so I lifted her frail body at 80 lbs. And said Jesus you have given me your son on Calvary So, I gave you, my daughter. Thank you for allowing me to have her for 39yrs.Suddenly, the Spirit of God spoke to me and said you have passed the test, now I know you are truly mean. Then I began to sing Amazing Grace. There were 5 police officers around her Body, and one was standing next to me. Tears was running down my face. The police said, do you realize this has never been before,5 police officers that are Spirit full here all at once. This is got to be God! I began to song. All at once all 5 police officers began to sing amazing grace. I began to sense the Spirit of God around use. Three days later, we landed our daughter Keetsie to rest.

The next morning, I started to get up and l fell to the floor I did not realize the impact it would have on my life till that day. I cried out help me mark. Mark run to see what was going on. Can you get up, I said I cannot walk so Mark took me to a doctor. The doctor checks me out and said, you have Lymphedema is a disease and there is no cure. I said to the doctor, this child will praise her God through this storm into my victory that my God has for me and thanking him for what I am walking through because I know than I will have the victory in becoming the child he has called me to be. It has been 9 years.

My Testimony

My husband and I moved to Reynoldsburg Ohio in 2010. A year later God begin to open doors for me to take over a healing ministry. In September, my daughter passed away. It was extremely hard on me, for she was my only daughter, and we were close; for we did everything together. The next Morning, I wake up, and as I was getting out of bed I fell to the floor. I called out to my husband Mark I cannot walk at that moment I realize losing my daughter Keetsie take a big toll in my life. My husband Mark took me to see a specialist Dr Goodyear. I ask him what was on my leg and said to me.

   This is what you would call a Lymphedema wart. It's a form of cancer. I am going to referred you to a physical therapist at OSU. Before you go, I will warp your legs to take down the swelling. I began to use a Lymphedema pump twice a day, which drew the toxins out of my body. I heard from my friend that Apostle Leon Walters was coming to town to minster at her church. That night Mark and I went to the service. Apostle Leon Walter's begun to speak on the power of God's healing anoint, he stops and look straight at me and said God said' you will live and not die.

   You will walk again, and you will dance again, for I have called you my Prophetess. The Lord said' you will do more than Katheryn Koulman, and you will walk into your destiny. I learned through my pain, and suffering, that through my trails to praise God, and whatever you go through; giving him thanks for this is the key to your victory in your life. James: 8. Count it all joy, when you go through trial for that were your victory

Birth Of El- Shaddai

One day I was looking to buy a home for my Husband, and I got tired of renting, so we were looking for a home on the internet and I saw this house for sale, and the Holy Spirit said that this was the one. I called the Realtor and said I would like to see this home for sale. She told me it was in contract' 'but you can see it, so we went to meet the Realtor at this house.

When we walked in this beautiful home, the Holy Spirit said to me, this is the one for I have chosen for you. You will call it, the home of EL-Shaddai Ministries. I looked at the Realtor and said this is my home. She laughed and said it is already in contract. I said God said this is my home.2 weeks later I got a call from the Realtor and said I do not know what happened "but if you know this home you can have it. I began to praise the Lord, and we moved in a week later. God is so faithful to his children. June 3rd, 2017; was the birth of the home of El-Shaddai ministries Columbus Ohio 80 people came to this event Pastors Prophetess, and Apostle. Came. Pastor Chad spoke, and said, as I approached the home of EL-Shaddai ministries he I saw the glory of God upon this home, was the fire of God burning on top of the roof. When I stepped out of the car, the power of God came all over me. I said this is Holy ground. About 30 minutes later A Prophetess approach me and said, Prophetess Cynthia; As I approached EL- Shaddai for the first time, and enter in this home, the Holy Spirit say that this property is a hedged roundabout by heaven Host, as this property is a portal of the lords, wherein angelic activity is free to be on earth as it is in heaven. This is the day that the home of EL-Shaddai ministers was born June 3rd, 2017.

God Delivers a Miracle

One day I made an appointment to see a cancer doctor, and her name was Dr. Backus. When I got there, I signed in and waited for them to call me in. After waiting for about 20 minutes, I was called in. They took me into a room and said here is a robe, put it on and Dr. Backus will be there within 5 minutes. Dr. Backus walked in and said Hi! How are you today? We talked a little bit, then she said Let us check you out. When doctor Backus was done, she said get dressed, then come to my office.

When I got there, I came in and set down. Dr. Backus began to tell me that I had stage 3 cancer, and had a 30% chance to make it through, and said I am so sorry, but you need to take chemo and radiation if you want to live. I looked at her and said not in your lifetime. Dr. Backus looked at me so funny, then I said ""My God will deliver this child from this. I will not receive those words, you gave me, for God will deliver me, as I am standing on his word, this child will walk through this storm in my life. Dr. Backus

He scheduled me for surgery a few weeks later. The day came for me to have my surgery; as I got there, I signed in. A nurse took me into a room prepping me. I was laughing and telling all the nurses and the people helping that my God will deliver me for I keep my eyes on Jesus. There were a couple of nurses that said it is so refreshing to see how you look at your situation, and the way you believe in your God. I wish more people could see through things like you do. I looked at them and said All you must do is ask Jesus into your heart and believe has a word with every fiber in your body and keeping your eyes on him.

Before they rolled me into surgery Dr. Backus came up to me and said are you ready! Yes, I am ready it was a couple of hours, then they rolled me out of surgery. and put me into a room to rest till I wake up. About 40 minutes later I wake up. A nurse came in and said I will make you an appointment to come back so Dr. Backus can check you out again in 6 months. The day came for my check up after surgery. I entered the room where Dr. Backus was waiting for me. As she was checking me out, I said my God is going to heal me. Dr Backus said we will, see? She had a puzzled look on her face and said, we will see. As Dr. Backus was checking me, she looked and said where the cancer is I cannot find it anywhere, it is as if you never had it. I said my God took it just as his word say, for God takes care of his children, who stand on his word with every fiber in her body, and never, waver, keeping on praising him through it all. Dr. Backus was speechless. I have been Cancer free for 5 years now. When God does it, he does it all the way.

God chose Dr. Backus because God wanted her to see that he is real. God gave me the best Doctor. Praise God. Mark & I walk back to the car Praise God for what he has done in my life. God's word will see you through. Just believe with every fiber in your body, and not waver' 'but stand on his word for it is food to the soul.

Encounter with God

Last Friday Morning when I got up and sat on the edge of the bed. I begin to sense the atmosphere change around and about me. As I got up and got dressed, and walked out into the dining area, and sat down. All sudden, I sense a cloud like a misty cloud with a silver lining; that was all around the library room in the hallway into the dining room. It was around me. It was such a wonderful sense of the presence of God. As I looked in the library room, I could see myself, and then I disappeared then I looked around the dining room; where I was sitting, and I could sense the cloud gathering all round me. It is such a peaceful moment, that something was about to take place.

My Spirit began to float upwards towards my heart as I looked up through the big window of my dining room, I saw Jesus on a white horse coming down close to my dining room window. My Spirit begins to rise even further up my neck. Jesus put his hand out and told my Spirit to go back down into my body, that it was not time, yet the Holy Spirit said, I could have taken you now, "but it is not time. I have allowed you to experience what will take place on that day. Then for people, they will experience the very thing that you have experienced. Look up my bride.

Many people in this world are wondering how they will know

when I come. Get ready people, for the Lord has spoken unto me to share with you, if anyone in the heart Jealousy, Attitude of this world, or Unforgiveness towards anyone, or thoughts in your mind that was not Holy will be judged, including, gossip, slander, corruption, communication, cursing, swearing, taking God's name in vain, speaking of evil, disobedience, witchcraft, love of self-greed, love of money complaining, and pornography; will not enter heaven. There is still time to turn your life over to Jesus.

What Wives Need to Know

I have learned in my 50 years of marriage when you want your husband to do something, allow him to have a space that is defined as his. Ask him respectfully, and with a pleasant tone of voice about projects you would like to be done around the house that you want them to do.

Do not nag at him to get the projects completed. Be clear in your request, do not make him guess. What he does is not up to your standards explain what you would prefer without being judgmental. Be his wife, not his mommy. Allow his input into what you are making for meals. Praise the things, that his accomplished.

Guard your tongue, as to how you talk about some things that you do not like in the house. He could take it as an attack on him or his ability to provide well for the family. Run your fingers through his hair and snuggle into his arms like a fluffy teddy bear, and that he is the man in your life.

God has a Purpose for You

God does not want us to waste our lives away. God wants us to live lives with purpose. God wants you to find your purpose in life, and not look at your past, but face the present. Then believe it!! for God has brought you through time and time again. I know in the Spirit he will do it again, for God loves you so much.

We have come into the New Year and as we reflect on 2019 leaving it behind and looking into the New Year, we need to remember to keep our focus, and fixes are eyes on Christ Jesus. No matter what happens in the next year, whether it brings great blessing or tough times; let us make sure to hold on, lean on and trust God more than anything in these troubled times. Christian are called to be on Spiritual standing strong, feet on the ground firm standing strong by the word, in the Spirit of God acts with courage, and to do everything in life.

Now I would like to share with you about the storm of life. There are storm's which manifest themselves in the secret places of the heart. What you and I need to remember today, as we face our own storms, it is because the Lord has sent us comfort. If just one of our lives is outside of his control, then we are in serious trouble. If Satan, the world or this flesh is able to-disrupt are lives apart from permission of God. Then no area of our life is safe.

However, If walking. Through the storms of this world. Believe in God. Read 2 Corinthians 4:15-15. For all things are for your sake, that the abundant grace might redound to the glory of God.18. While we look not all the things which are seen: but at things which are not seen: for the things which are seen are temporal: but the things which are not seen are eternal. John 14:3 And if I go and prepare a place for you. I will come again and receive you unto myself: that "where Am there ye may be also. KJV 1st Thessalonians 4:13-18 But I would not have you to be ignorant, concerning them which are asleep, that ye sorrow not, even as others which have no hope. For if we believe that Jesus died and rose again, even so them also which sleep in Jesus will God bring with him. For this we say unto you by the word of the Lord, that we which are alive and remain unto the coming of the Lord shall not prevent them which are sleep. For the Lord himself shall descend from heaven with a shout, with the voice of the archangel, and with the trump of God: and the dead in Christ shall rise first: Then we which are alive and remain shall be caught up together with them in the clouds, to meet the Lord in the air: and so, shall we ever be with the Lord.

Wherefore comfort one another with these words. KJV) Mark6:-13. And he went out from thence, and came into his own country, and his disciples followed him. And when the sabbath day came, he began to teach in the synagogue: and many hearing him were astonished saying from whence hath this man these things? And what wisdom is this which is given unto him, that even such mighty works are wrought by his hands? Is not this the carpenter, the son of Mary, brother of James, and Jo's-es,and of Judah, and Simon and are not his sisters here with us? And they were offended at him.

But Jesus said unto them A prophet is not without honor, but in his own country and among his own kin, and in his own house. 'And he could do no mighty work, have that he laid his hands upon a few sick folks, and healed them. And 'he marveled because of their unbelief 'And he went round about the villages teaching. And he called unto him the twelve and began to send them forth by two and two; and gave them power over unclean spirits; And commanded them that they should take nothing for their journey, save a staff only; no script, no bread, no money in their purse: But be shod with sandals; and not put on two coats. And he said unto them, in what place soever ye enter a house, there abide till ye depart from that place. And whosoever shall not receive you, nor hear you, when ye depart thence, shake off the dust under your feet for a testimony against them. Verily I say unto you, it shall be more tolerable for Sodom and Gomorrah on the day of judgment, than for that city. And they went out and preached those men should repent. And they cast out many devils, and anointed with oil many that were sick, and healed them.

When we are not walking in faith, he is not able to use us in the way he would like to. If you are in the storm today in your life, you need to know that God can calm your storm in your life.

Seeing through the eyes of God

To see through the eyes of God is to see Christ as he sees us with an unconditional love. Do you know as humans; we tend to focus on our problems that surround us. The devil will do everything at that point to make it seem like a demanding situation that we cannot overcome. When we stop seeing the problem around us and start seeing the solutions with our spiritual eyes, of faith, then we will begin to have a Godly outlook.

We need to see his healing virtues, his unfailing love, his mercy that endures to all generations and having the father's heart. Have you ever thought about how God sees when he looks at us? He sees how different people have helped and hurt you. He sees our disappointment our fear's our failures, and how all these things have changed us in a good, or bad way. His desire is to be greater than ourselves; at the same time God sees how we can be our worst enemy. God sees that we are doing the best we can, though he knows we can do better. God sees our wishes for love and Success.

God also sees that we are searching for answers, but we do not really know the way, because we are getting in the way of God. Our problems, our selfishness, our earthly vanities, our anxieties, our lack of trust ... We are all like a closed curtain on a window. They prevent us from seeing what the Holy Spirit would have us to see. 'But the truth is as people, we really do not want to see all God wants us to see, because we are afraid to see the truth. We really know that if we could see the truth of God ... Then we would have to act on those truths and many of us are not ready for that yet.

To see with the eyes of God, we are first must God and when you understand how God sees us, we can look at our neighbors, and finally understand what God sees in each, and every one of us. I Samuel 16:7. You see God measures man by his divine standard, for God sees not as man sees, for man looks at the outward appearance, but the Lord looks at the past, and are outward man, and looks past possessions, and costly attire; he studies the heart, every thought and desire. You see God does not judge by how tall we may stand, or how much we oppose, or the rank we endure. God will honor the man who keeps his heart pure. For the eyes of God are searching to and froe, we have no secrets that our God does not know our father knows our thoughts. God understands every part of our life. Man sees the outside, "But God see the heart. When we begin to see the world as God sees it, we will begin to understand. To love like God is to hope like God, and his desire is that you love him. God wants you to tell the world about the goodness of God, and what he is to you. God's heart cries out for his children. His desire is to do them good, and not evil. Life we tend to write people off and wash our hands of people.

That is not God's way, and it certainly does not show who he is. Love cries and longs for people to understand. It calls out to those who are lost, and comforts those who are hurting. Love is an Enabler. It's enables people to overcome, to and to see clearly. It enables people to see God inside of their institution.

Your reflection of love is what enables the people in your circle of influence to see God, for who he really is in you. When you look through the eyes of God you will see a hurting and dying world. With the eyes of God. Whenever we can't understand what we are seeing, we are able to begin to reason or not try to figure it out ourselves. When we begin to pray and allow God to help us see through his eyes, then God will give you peace that floods your soul. Those wonderful miracles are God's gift that we must cling to, and to be grateful for them and surrender everything else in your life to God. If we could see as God sees we would be able to understand, that no trail comes without a spiritual fight.

Question?

Through the eyes of people, do they see a reflection of who God is in your life?

God has given us his Holy Spirit that allows us to see through the eyes of faith and be steadfast in your walk of faith. When we are guided by God's Spirit, he will never lead us astray.

What makes you Live

What the world needs are people, who have come alive in God. Everything you have missed; you have gained something more. Everything you gain you lose something else. The doors we open, and close each decide the lives we shall live. It Hurts to love someone, and not be loved in return, but what is most painful is to love someone, and never find the courage to let that person know how you feel. One day your life will flash before your eyes.

Make sure it is worth watching to love is to risk not being loved in return. To hope is to risk pain. To try is to risk failure, but risk must be taken, because the greatest hazard in life is to risk nothing. Our attitude toward life determines life's attitude toward us. The difference between school, and life. In school you are taught a lesson, and then given a test. In life you are given a text which teacher is you a lesson.

Life is not measured by the number of breaths we take but by the moments that take our breath away. Memory is a way of holding on to the things you love, the things you never wanted to lose. Our eyes need to be washed by are tear, once in a while, so that we can see life with a clearer view. Looking life through the rear-view mirror.

This means looking forward in life, never looking back at

your past; for it will stop you from having what God has for you. Life is the art of drawing without an eraser. God has for you a Life is the art of drawing without an eraser. God asks no man whether he will accept life, but that is not the choice you must take it. The only question is how. Whatever God takes you through, God will see you through it. Live as if today was your last day. Live as if you were to live forever.

Laugh as much as you breath, and love if you live. God can give you a new beginning starting today and make it a new ending. Every ending is a new beginning. If you want a happy ending, that depends of course, where you stop your life story.

Learning how to win in your life

I would love to share with you, what I have learn in life. I pray that this will help you on your journey of life with God. When we live in hate or forgiveness they win. If you live in the victim's story, they win. If you want to win, you must focus on building your future in Jesus, and start right now. I learned to with the help of the Holy Spirit to release the weight from my pass, and lay it on Jesus' feet, so I can be free. You can do it too.

Do not allow events of the past, which are now gone, to ruin this moment, which is now to enjoy, what Jesus has for you, which is ready for you to live fully. Do not allow other people's opinions and judgment to control the direction of your life! They want you to go down your past you don't want to travel. People who like to please people to get what they want is a curse, that should be avoided at all costs. Before you do anything; ask because of fear of judgment from others. You were born to stand out, and to be appreciation, and loved for who you are in Christ Jesus. Do not dim your light so you fit into the dull background of other people lives. Shine with the glory of God that is upon your life as you are, and those who really care for you will see that light will shine with in you.

Do not allow your life to be controlled by people. Do you know that many people spend their lives at the mercy of circumstance's?

Living at the mercy of what happens to them. Living at the mercy of other people. Not living in the present, because they are stuck in the prison of their past. If you want to live a GREAT LIFE don't allow yourself to be controlled by any of these things Your past. Other people's opinions and Judgment's Limited beliefs you project on yourself and Relationships and money Don't allow your past to control your Present or future life. Whatever happens you must let it go. Leave the pain of your pass behind so it cannot ruin your future. Leave the darkness of your past behind, so it cannot block the light of your bright future.

Your past is gone for Jesus throw it into the sea of forgiveness cover by the blood of Jesus. Whatever happened whether unjust, cruel, harsh, words whatever the case. If someone, did you wrong, the only way you can win, is if you let go and move on forgive them for, they know not went they do. Nothing outside, that can hold you back your entire life will change the very instant you very instant you decide to change to change your mindset. The instant you decide to see everything as a gift from God. When you decide to see every circumstance, and challenge as a blessing rather than a curse, the very instant you become conscious to the fact; that everything is as it should be. Do not allow your life to control you by your own limited beliefs. Now these beliefs may be conscious, but more than likely they are unconscious.

They may be unconditional in your entire life by listening to those around you, as we reach out to are dreams. Notice your own limited beliefs is telling them to shut up There is nothing you cannot do. NOTHING you cannot have. If you believe in Christ. If you believe anything is POSSIBLE. When you change your belief from limited to unlimited in Christ Jesus your potential is unlimited. Imagine what you could achieve, if you lived a life; that God has given you, as although Miracles are requirement of everyday life.

The Call

One night as I was sitting, and watching a Christian movie suddenly, the Spirit of God came upon me so strong; I could not move. Tears being to flow down my face. The glory of God was all around me, and the Spirit said My daughter I have chosen you to walk the walk of Moses, to walk in the shoes of Moses, for I will do heart and mighty things through you, for I have given you a rare calling, only few dares to walk that narrow road, for I will be by your side. The next Morning, I knew that I was different. I felt God's presence like never I heard my phone.

I pick up my phone Hello good Morning. It was my friend. Sandy wanted me to know there will be a special speaker coming to their church, so Mark and I went that evening. In the middle of the service this Lady name Patty stood and looked at the speaker, and said, the Spirit of God has a word as she turns round, and pointed at me and said, you in the back role the lady in the pink? What is your name Cynthia, God is showing me a candy cane, and on this candy cane the stripe began to unfold, and straighten out completely?

Then the candy cane began to turn red, there were no more white areas. The Lord wanted you not to use this as a cane. "But as a staff like noses did to lead his people out of bondage. The

Spirit of God said, I have given you a staff to bring signs and wander to my people to set them free from bondage. I have chosen you as a Moses. I have called you the narrow path that few walk. Go as my Prophetess, that I your God!! For I will be with you.

The Eyes of God

To see through the eyes of God is to see Christ as he sees us with an unconditional love. Do you know as humans; we tend to focus on our problems, that surround us. The devil everything at the point to make it seem a tricky situation, that we cannot over Come. When we stop seeing the problem around us, and start seeing the solutions with our Spiritual eyes, of interfaith we will begin to have a Godly outlook. We need to see his healing virtues, his unfailing love, his mercy that endures to all generations, and having the father's heart. Have you ever looked through a hole? When God looks at us what does he see? He sees how different people has helped and hurt you. He sees our disappointments, our fear's our failures, and how all these things have changed us in a good, or bad way. His desire is to be greater than ourselves; at the same time God sees how we can be our worst enemy. God can see that we are doing the best we can, though he knows we can do better. God can see our wishes for love and success.

God also can see; that we are searching for answers but do not really know where to find it, because we are getting in the way of God. Our problems our self-greed, our earthly vanities, our anxieties our lack of trust ... We are all like a closed curtain on a window. They prevent us from seeing what the Holy Spirit would have us to see. "But the truth is … as people, we really do not want to see all God wants us to see, because we are afraid to see truth. We really know that if we could see the truth of God …

Then we would have to act on those truths and many of us are not quite ready for that yet. In order, to see with the eyes of God, we must first -see God, and when you understand how God see us, we can look at our neighbors, and finally understand what God sees in each, and every one of us. I Samuel 16:7 you see God measures man by his divine standard, for God sees not as man. Man sees, for man looks at the outward appearance, but the Lord looks at the past and outward man looks possession and looks post possession and costly attire; he studies the heart, every thought, and desire.

You see God does not judge by how tall we stand, or how much we possess, or the rank we command, and the title we hold. His gaze goes far deeper to things; that endure. God will honor the man who keeps his heart pure, for the eyes of the Lord are searching to and for, we have no secrets; that our God does not know. Our father knows our thoughts, and though, and God-understands every part of our life. Man sees the outside, 'but does see the heart. When we begin to see the world as God sees it; we will begin to understand. To love like God is to hope like God, and his desire is that you love him. God wants you to tell the world about the goodness of God, and what he has for you. God's heart cries out for his children. His desire is to do them good and not evil. Life we tend to write people off and washing is in the hands of people.

That is not God's way, and it certainly does not show who he is. Love cries, and comforts those who are hurting. Love is an Enabler. It enables people to overcome and see clearly. It enables people to see God inside of their situation. Your reflection of love is what enables the people in your circle of influence to see God for who he really is in you. When you look through the eyes of God, you will see a hurting, and dying world. With the eyes of God. Whenever we cannot understand what we are seeing and are able to begin to reason or not trying to figure it out ourselves.

When we begin to pray, and allow God to help us see his eyes, then God will give you peace that floods your soul. Those wonderful miracles are God's gift's that we must cling to, and to be grateful for them, and surrender everything else in your life to God. Therefore, we now have an instrument of peace, and a healing in our life. If we could see as God see's we would be able to understand, that no trail comes without a spiritual fight.

Arms of God

Jesus right now at this moment has poured his love upon you, like you have never known. You sense God's arms wrap all round you, with such pure love from heaven. The angels are all around you, bringing has peace upon your body, telling you it's okay to stay in the father's arms, for he is putting his glory upon you.

He has seen your hurt and pain and people that has miss understood you that you have walk through in your life. My child my arms are open wide to you for I have never left you, for I have always been here for you.

The Biggest Lesson

The Biggest lesson I have learned on my journey is you cannot please everyone you see. Life is like an elevator on your way up, sometimes you have to stop, and let some people off; because they would you back from what God wants for you, and sometimes change is exactly what we need saying goodbye is the hardest thing 'but the best thing. One of the hardest lessons Whether it is guilt, anger, love, loss, or betrayal change is never easy, but we fight to hold on, and we fight to let go. The hardest battles are those, which we fight inside, especially those, which we fight silently with a smile on our face. These battles often leave scars too deep to see from outside. Real victory is in healing to those scars with time and living again in the eyes of God.

This is what life will teach you

Anything-that has power over you is teaching you patience, patience, and when someone abandons you, it is teaching you how to stand up on your own two feet. Anything; that angers you is teaching you forgiveness, and compassion. Anything that has power over you is teaching you. It is teaching you how to take your power back. Anything you hate is teaching you unconditional love. Anytime you cannot control is teaching you how to let go.

What your complaint's actually reveal about your heart.

You know when You know when we try not to speak negative, but it still happened. We began to grumble and complain that people do not like to be around complainers, and yet we slide down that slippery slope after we like to admit it. It is a heart not of God. Do you know that the has lot to say about anger? I do not mean rightness anger we experience towards injustice or evil, but sinful anger knows many times we may feel we are righteous in our anger because someone wronged us anger often involves our sense of justice, but it is extremely easy to slide into sinful anger?

Here are some biblical truth and principles that God must help us make progress in anger is nor caused by other people or our circumstance comes out of your heart. In Mathew 15:19— For out of the heart comes proceed evil thoughts, murders, adulteries evil thoughts of murder, thought of fornication's thefts, false witness, blasphemies:

Believe it or not, your circumstances do not cause you to anger. Anger is your own sin. Are heart beings like a sponge? If black comes out of it or clear water comes out of it. What does this mean?

People and circumstance can squeeze our hearts, and if anger comes out, it is because that's what was in our heart. Have you ever noticed that when we try not to speak negatively but still do and yet we slide down that slippery slide moving more offer than we like to admit? It is not of God because I know many times, we may feel we are righteous in us and are angry because someone wronged us. Anger often involves our sense of justice, but it's extremely easy to hear some biblical truth, and principles that God must help us make progress.

life is a wonder

Anything that annoys you is teaching you patience. Anyone who abandons you is teaching you how to stand up on your own two feet. Anyone that angers you.

God doesn't want us to waste our lives away. God wants us to live everyday of our lives with purpose. God wants you to find your purpose in life, and not look at your past, but face the present. Then believe it! For God has brought you through time and time again. I know in the Spirit he will do it again, for God loves you so much. We have come into the New year as we reflect on 2019 leaving it behind and living in the year of 2020. We need to remember to keep our focus, and fixes are eyes on Christ Jesus. No matter what happens in the next year, whether it brings great blessing or tough times; let's make sure to hold on, lean on and trust God more than anything in these troubled times.

Christians are called to be on spiritual standing strong, feet on the ground firm standing by the word, in the Spirit of God acts with courage, and to do everything in life. Now I would like to share with you about the storms of life. There are storms in homes, Marriages at work, and at churches; these are storm's which manifest themselves in the secret places of the heart. What you and I need to remember today, as we face our own.

God's Clouds

Why does the scripture include that statement about a cloud receiving Jesus when he ascended? If it were a normal cloud-Jesus would have ascended "into a cloud. Scripture says that a cloud received him. Let us look in Act 1:8-9. But ye shall receive power, after that the Holy Ghost is come upon you: and ye shall be witnesses unto me both in Jerusalem, and in all Judea, and in Samara, and unto the uttermost part of the earth. And when he had spoken these things, while they beheld, he was taken up; and a cloud received him out of their sight. To me that indicate that the cloud had some abilities to accept Jesus.

Paul tells us about how Jesus will be returning bringing all his saints. In Theses 3:13. He will return bringing with him those who have been washed by the lamb of God .. What do you see in your clouds? In Revelation 1:7 said "Behold? He cometh with clouds. In the Bible—Clouds are always connected with God. Clouds are those sorrow or suffering within or without our personal lives which seem to dispute the rule of God. It is by those very clouds, that the Spirit of God. It is by those very clouds, that the Spirit of God is teaching us how-to walk-in faith.

If there were no clouds, we would not have any faith. "The clouds are but the dust of our father's feet. The clouds are a sign not true to say, which God wants to teach us something in our trails: and through them he is there. What a revelation it is to know that sorry, and suffering are the clouds,' that comes along with God. God cannot come near without clouds; he does not come in clear shining. It is every cloud he brings; he wants us to unclean something in your life. His purpose in the clouds is to simplify our relief until our relationship to him is exactly, then of a child. It is the relationship between you and God getting simpler than ever it has been.

There is a connection between the strange divine ways of God, and what we have to learn to interpret by the mysteries of life in the light of our knowledge of God, unless we can look darkness fully in face without amazing God's character, and we do not yet know him. Are you for the day or are you living for life eternal? Are you going to care for the opinion of men here? Or the opinion of men won't avail us much. When we get before the judgment throne room of God. God talks about the clouds, for in the gospels saying how Jesus will come in the clouds with the clouds of heaven. John did not mention in his gospel 'But John did in his book of Revelation.

Those clouds of heaven ae also mention in the Old Testament scripture Daniel on them, saying and behold with the clouds of heaven. One like a son of man was coming, and he came up to the Ancient of days, and was presented before him. Daniel 7:13. I saw in the night visions, and behold, one like the Son of man came with the clouds of heaven, and came to the Ancient of days, and they brought him near before him. The scripture says something might help us understand what Jesus is telling us. The fallen asleep in Jesus will raise up the bodies of the dead in Christ. The saints will be coming back with Jesus, and their bodies will be resurrected. Jesus will resurrect the faithful, who are still living at that time. Ezekiel 1: He saw storm cloud, and a bright light, continuous flashing fire. Ezekiel. Also said; As the appearance of the rainbow in the clouds on a rainy day, and such was the appearance of the likeness of the glory of the Lord.

Question

Was Ezekiel fore teller? The Lord return in his glory Cloud? YES!!! Read Luke 17:25 for Jesus was speaking through Ezekiel for Ezekiel was seeing Jesus coming on the clouds of the sky. Read 11

Thessalonians1:10 And to wait for his Son from heaven, whom he raised from the dead, even Jesus,

even Jesus, which delivered us from the wrath to come.

What is Radical faith

Do you know what radical faith is? It is active and acting on God's word. One needs to confess. Matthew, it said from the days of John the Baptist, until now the kingdom of heaven suffers violence, and the violence takes it by force. What does this mean?

It is a force faith that is needed to obtain the Kingdom benefits, because Satan was given certain dominion in the world; when Adam failed, but Christ came to break Satan's power and power to restore God's authority on earth.

Jesus said in Ephesians for this through the obedience, and faith of God's followers. In Mathew 16: 17- 19; Jesus said the gates of Hell shall not prevail against you. In Proverbs 4: 20-22 it said If you confess out loud; for they are life to those who find their health to all their flesh. Did you know never say My cancer, or My arthritis, or whatever, you confess with your mouth, you are claiming possession of that disease. Do not refer to them as yours, but something the Devil is trying to put on you. Do not accept them, and don't sign that package.

Trials of life

In II Samuel 16:7 say The Lord does not look at the things the way man looks at them. Man looks at the outward appearance "But the Lord looks at heart. In Luke 16:15 said, and he said to them, you are they which justify yourselves before men: But God knows your hearts, for the highly esteemed among men is abomination in the sight of God. God knows whether you have chosen too fellow him or to fellow Satan.

Question?

Then what is the purpose of the test God sends our way?

If God already knows where we stand, and the benefits from the test, so he can see how much we love him. We are the ones who benefit. We may claim to believe, and we might think we follow our savior 'but until we have to stand with him in the face of a trial, we will never know the power of God. Romans 5;2. By whom also we love access by faith into this Grace wherein we stand and rejoice in hope of the Glory of God. We must also keep in mind that; we have been given the right to choose in hope of the Glory of God. We must also keep in mind that we have been given the right to choose. In

Proverbs 16:1-8. In Hebrews 11:17-19 says Abraham considered the command a sentence of death.

He intended to carry it out. He believed God would raise Isaac from the dead, if necessary. God knew Abraham's faith without putting Abraham and Isaac through this pain but notice the statement; that he stood in faith and pass the test. Genesis 22:7 said, And Isaac spoke unto Abraham his father, and said, my father: and said, my father and he said, here am I, my son, and he said, Behold the fire and the wood: but where is the lamb for a burnt offering? And Abraham said, my son, God will provide himself a lamb for a burnt offering: so they went both of them together. came unto his father, and he said 'Here am I, my son of the living God. Abraham, or Isaac or anyone else be sure, that Abraham who raised the knife would carry out God's command? We talk about the great faith of Abraham "But we cannot see Abraham's mind.

We recognize his faith by the deeds recorded for us. Romans 4:16-25 said, therefore is of faith, that it might by Grace to the end the promise might be sure to all the seed, not only those; which are of the law, but to that also; which is of the faith of Abraham who is the father of us all. Verse 25 said Who was delivered because of offenses, and were raised because us did tempt Abraham, and said unto him. Abraham when he was tried, offered up Isaac: and he who received the promise offered up his only begotten son. Verse 18 says of whom it was said, that in Isaac shall your seed be called. Abraham and Isaac went through this pain, 'but notice the statement: that he stood in faith and passed the test. Abraham considered the command a sentence of death. He intends to carry it out. Abraham raised the knife to carry out God's command. Abraham could have declared his faith in God from every housetop, but if had failed to sacrifice his son, he would have failed the test.

We too may declare our faith in Jesus; but if we cannot perform the simple act of being baptized for mission of our sins, and then we to have failed the test. He believed that God could raise Isaac from the dead, if necessary. Verse 19 said Accounting the God was able to raise him up from the dead whence also he received him in a figurative sense. We may claim to be believers, and we may think we follow our savior, but until we have stood with him in the face of a trial, we will never know the power of God. Romans 5;2 Said by whom also we have access by faith into this grace in which we stand and rejoice in hope of the glory of God We must also keep in mind that; we are free moral agents. We have been given the right to choose. Abraham's offering of Isaac was a test of God. Geneses 22;1 Say and it happened after these things, that God test Abraham and said to him, 'Abraham and he said, Here AM, In Hebrew 11:17-19 say, Abraham considered the command a sentence of death. He intended to carry it out. He believed God would raise Isaac from the dead if necessary. God know Abraham's faith without putting Abraham, and Isaac through this pain, but notice the statement that he stood in faith, and pass the test. Genesis 22:7 said. And Isaac came unto his father and said my father and he said "Here am I, my son.

Could Abraham, or Isaac or anyone else be sure that Abraham who raised the knife would carry out God's command? We talk about the great faith of Abraham 'but we cannot see Abraham, but we cannot see Abraham mind. We recognize his faith by the deeds recorded for us. Romans 4:16-25 said, Therefore, it is of faith, that it might by grace to the end the promises might be sure to all the seed, not only those which are of the law, but to that also which is of the faith of Abraham who is the father of us all. Verse 25 said, who was delivered, because of offense, and were raised, because our justification, this means that raised up with him in newness of life. We recognize his faith by the deeds recorded for use. Abram could have declared his faith in God from every housetop, 'but if he failed to sacrifice his son, he would have failed the test. We may declare our faith in Jesus, 'but if we cannot perform the simple act of being baptized for the remission of our sin, then we to fail the test. If we as of being baptized for the remission of our sin, then we to fail the test. If we as Christians ask for forgiveness, God will forgive us and will pick us up and try again. God will make him to stand. In this way, the trail will purify us by fire. Peter1:6-7, said view your trials as an opportunity to show where you stand, to find out what you too need to work on.

Trusting the winds of God

When trusting the winds of God; we can soar on the winds of God. The Holy Spirit is the wind of God. He has been given to us to lead us into all truth. When God's people praise him; it causes the wind to blow, and the current of the breath of God to blow again and lift us up.

What a lesson for God's children to learn how often do we waste are strength by jumping out too soon, instead of waiting on God's direction so we can soar to new heights and fly to places unknown; rather than seeking solutions to our problems, many of us complain about them to anyone; that will listen. We cannot see a solution to our problems, because we are so busy flapping around like the eagles. What we do not realize is that the problems are in our lives, so that we can learn to fly.

When you realize that God will catch you from dying, when you take, that step of faith; you will develop that deep abiding faith in God that allows us to learn to raise above our problems, and soar like the Eagles, when we trust God to help us rise above our problems, we begin to see clearly are solutions. When we see that occurs in our lives even our problem is for our highest, and greatest good. Problems come into our lives to help us grow and learn to come closer to God, and without them, we would sit in the comfort of our nest and never learn to Fly. God is calling you too good. and wonderful things of God.

God needs every eagle health so, that this nation can be reached. Abraham had the faith, and patience and, held onto the p0romise that God gave him. We must hold onto are promises of God, and the healing power of God is at work in your life; for he crowns you with living kindness and tender mercies and grace. This is the character of God of God gives us a crowned and to receive the holy Spirit. I pray that God will teach us to set our hops on him and help us to hold on firmly to the promise of eternal life, and that the love' that God has put into our hearts weren't put their two stays because love isn't love till you give it away. Romans 5:5 says God's love has been poured into our hearts without measure pray that you will not only receive Gods love and strength but his grace and God righteousness and his abundance in your life.

Life is like a breath of air

Have you ever told friends and family that you love them or how you appreciate them or thinking about them and loving them, because they have poured into your life and made it better, while they are still on Earth? Do you know why we fail? It is because we don't try hard enough, pressing through; and persevering because trying always leads to success regardless of the outcome because God is leading you through.

Through our mistakes and failures, we receive strength and wiser teaching us that only through God we can learn how to truly live through the eyes of God? In the end only one thing makes a dream impossible to achieve, and that's the failure to try. The results are not based on what you plan to do, or what you'll do. Your results come from what you try and do consistently. Our lives get better, because we are investing in ourselves; mentally, physically, and spiritually it a priority to learn, to grow positively everyday if you stick to it.

The stronger you become in God, the more wonderful our life will become. This alone will require much patience. It means that doing what has been made available to you, while understanding that the results you seek are worth the time and effort; you see patience is the realization that the quality of things that you fill your life with. Patience is willingness to accept and appreciate what you have right now, while you put forth the effort in focusing and growing towards your dreams and goals.

With the power and strength of God leading you into what he has for you. We know the best things in life are not actual things. Things in life. Relationship experiences your relationship and meaning you know meaning you know meaning you know humans are not perfect, there are times where we have lost patience, our tempers, and our attitude misplaces.

Life isn't about a single triumph. It's about the trials and errors that get you there. Do you know what? It will matter in the end; for every step, regrets, decisions, afflictions that we face. The only way we will make it through the grace of God as we walk close with our lord and savior. During your walk with God, you will be strengthened for God will lead you to every success you've never had. All of this has made you who you are today.

Though you have been broken down many times; keep in mind how remarkable that is, and how you are in the palms of God's hands, we grow stronger having learned of God's love. In return we will find the strength in God growing through the storms. I think the most important thing as Christians we should do.

We should show the world God's love through us. Through our storms we can show God's kindness and wisdom in this crazy world that we live in, because God holds us close in his arms. God will fight your battle and arrange the things in your favor. In return making a way even when you don't see it as we live the life God has given us.

Having the peace in your life

When we wait upon the Lord God; he is shaping and preparing us for something so amazing and wonderful in our life, that we would not have otherwise. We have never seemed to be able to recognize the wait in our lives as being part of something of positive value. We see this as an inconvenience or interruption onto our activities in life.

Most of the things that really matter in life are not going to happen in just a minute, such as, when the traffic light holds us up when no one else is coming in the opposite direction or waiting in the long line at the grocery store. They come for those who learn to wait upon him. To wait upon the lord means to simply let God be God.

It means to acknowledge God's lordship over the time in our lives and learning the lesson of patience. God offers the promise of renewing our spirit. Sometimes life demands more than just recharge. God is ready to exchange our failing strength, for his unfailing energy.

In (KJV) Isaiah it talks about giving his power to the weak, and those who have no might. God will increase our strength, for he promises to give those who wait upon him in all our circumstances in life. God directs our lives to determine the rhythm of life it is letting God be God in our lives. In every true Christian believer.

God has prepared his children with divine strength in our lives, that only comes from heaven. Many of us however are unaware of the available strength that comes from God; but we simply do not know the way to receive it. If our work is to bring blessings to others. It will depend entirely upon our waiting on the Lord. Sometimes we are weary from the constant work, and from despair, and failure; but we are never weary in the spirit.

Why? Because we are being cared on by the Joy of almighty God! God loves us and carries about us. All you need to do is trust and obey him in every area of your life. Then you will have peace in your life, that you have never known.

God's Unconditional Love

In (KJV)1 John 4:19 said- We love him, because he first loved us. If a man says, I love God, and hated his brother, he is a liar: for he that loveth not his brother whom he hath seen, how can he love God whom he hath not seen? There are thousands of people who speak of the unconditional love of God; would discover the biblical "meaning" of what they say, if that happened many would find their feet on solid ground.

Is your lifelong love possible? Yes! For love is not just a feeling love is not an emotion. Love is a choice to look past the flaws, forgive the failure's, to glance over the imperfection, and investigate the heart. Love is a choice and a command. A new command I give to you Love. (KJV) John 3:16 For God so loved the world, that he gave his only begotten Son, that whosoever believe in him should not perish, but have everlasting life. Is lifelong love possible? Absolutely! We must put others' needs above our own.

God loves you and offers a wonderful plan for your life. One of the greatest mistakes that we make is that we measure God's love for us by our present circumstances. When we think of things that are going bad for us, we usually assume that God works only through the success we have in our lives, and not through our weaknesses. The truth is that our circumstances are constantly changing, but God's love is always with us. His love for you and me does not ride on the waves of our feelings.

We also bring many unwanted circumstances on ourselves, and because of ones usually responsible for many of those problems that we often find ourselves in. It is hard for us to understand that if God really loves us, then exactly what is his purpose for allowing so many dreadful things to come into our lives. Having faith in God does not mean that trusting God to stop the bad storms in our lives. Faith and trust in God are things which enable us to walk through those periods of hurt and sorrow and come out victorious.

We must trust God and believe that when trouble occurs, he is going to give us the ability to cope with it. We often wonder why? God loves us then why? Doesn't he answer our prayers immediately? Please remember that God can see the total picture. When we work hard for him, he loves us and when we don't work hard, he still loves us because we are his creation. When we show God our love, we spend time with his in prayer and when we thank him for not only for the blessings that he bestows upon us, but also, we are thankful to him when he has to correct and chastise us due to sin. Stay in the righteous path. Ask God to show you what to do in certain situations, it shows a great deal of love, respect, and trust within God.

God has sent that Holy Spirit into your life. Teaching us instructions to you about him and his ways. You will soon find that a wonderful love is flowing back and forth between you and your God. Please remember that true love of God requires an investment in the things of eternal value. True love requires a true conviction and a desire to know and experience his love beyond all this world could ever offer.

You are God's Daughter

God wants you to know; you are a daughter of the highest, a Holy Princess, a woman with. Of whom we are as daughters of the king, this faces we present to the world. We must remove are mask my sisters. We as woman have suffered through the years with insecurity and betrayal because of this, the fallen in trap of pretending to be someone they were never created or called to be. It is as though they are hiding behind a mask. Without a true understanding of who we are as daughters of the King, the faces we present to the world may not be who we really are is underneath. If we are to be Princess warriors; that were meant to be.

We must remove the mask. It is only than we will be equipped to help another woman remove the mask that they are hiding. Do you know that every woman passionately in love with Jesus is so priceless a warrior, who shows the glory of God upon their face to this dying world? God always purification process from one stage of lives to the next. God purifies us through his word, trails, and tests. God wants to see if we are ready to stand the process. It's during this process; that we ask the question. 'Who am I really here for? You see the enemy wants to stop you from fulfilling your destiny and does not want you to truly realize your full potential or the gifts, and talents "that God has place inside you, because he knows if you find out he knows his able to stop.

Man and Woman of God

When God comes and lives in us, where we go, the kingdom goes with us. When we speak! Heaven speaks. Am a Christ Am ambassador, I am omnipotent, and appointed for action. The best years are upon you. You are going from glory to glory. I pray that you are ready for what God has for you. How do you keep your marriage strong and healthy?

My husband Mark have found that first thing we do in the morning, and at night before we turn in, then we ask God to come upon us with strength foe that day. It brings us closer together as we pray for each other every day. We pray over each other for God to give us favor and bless us each day, and then say, I love you.

We leave in our drawers for are spouse to find and read. Our love and our affection goes beyond the physical realm into the emotional, and spiritual realm. This develops true intimacy with each other, and with God. We never go to bed angry but take each other's hand to pray for God's forgiveness then forgive each other. We set aside time every morning to read the bible together.

We also read to each other from the word of God, that he would have for are mate. It brings a wonderful intimate time of strengthening in our marriage. This keeps the romantic love alive and will also be a bold testimony to strength your Christian marriage. This will keep your marriage at the feet of Jesus when you show respect by showing it.

1. Each person cherishes the other
2. Each finds pleasure and the comfort.
3. Emotional support of each other.
4. View that each partner is special in some important way.
5. A feeling of safety friendship, and trust.
6. The sense that each partner is blessed to have each other.
7. We balance each other.
8. An ability to express both positively and negative emotions.
9. Hold hands; At least unexpected time and surprise.
10. Leave love notes around the home, in the car, your spouse bag.
11. Take a vacation just you and your spouse, even if it's just one night away at a local hotel.
12. Surprise your spouse by flirting, you know you used to do it.
13. Make your bedroom a sanctuary, that is special for you both.
14. Make it a place where you can get away, where you can feel at peace and at rest.
15. Say I love you.
16. Text your honey or sweetheart a special message just for him or her. Let them find it after work.
17. Make love. Pray together, because once you star praying, you will start to feel closer to each other having faith and supporting, faith can make the difference between each other.
18. Being able to keep a marriage or losing it.

19. While it may take energy, and courage' that seem unavailable in times where stress has used up all available resources, digging down deep to sustain your faith will, in the end, swill result a payoff of a hundredfold.

The payoff comes into long run, when surviving the rough times, that strengthens the marriage, and your faith. In a way, it is like a bone, which breaks, then heals the fracture because, it is the strongest part of the bone. So too, a marriage can survive tough times. Once you overcome, the problems, it will become a source of strength to the marriage, and to your faith. Your marriage can become one of great satisfaction, and enduring love, but it will take lots of work, and a commitment to staying in the marriage even through the rough times, but it will be the marriage' that God intention it to be.

God's timing

Let us talk about God's timing. The first thing we need to understand about God's timing is that it is perfect, just as all God's ways are perfect. Let's look in Psalm 18:30 As for God, his way is perfect: the word of the Lord is tried: he is a buckler to all those that trust in him. God's timing is never early, and it's never been late.

Patience is a spiritual fruit. Galatians 5:22 But the fruit of the Spirit is love, joy, peace, long suffering, gentleness, goodness such there is no law. In the scripture makes it clear, that God is please with us when we display this virtue, be still before the Lord, and wait patiently for him. Psalm 37:7 said s Rest in the Lord, and fret not thyself because of him who prosper in his way, because of the man who brings wicked devices to pass. Lamentations 3:25 said The Lord is good unto them that wait for him, to the soul that seethe him see when we have patience often reveals the degree of trust we have in God's timing. We should take great comfort in knowing that, when we wait on the Lord, we receive divine energy and strength; But those who wait on the Lord shall renew their strength; they shall walk and not faint.

The Season of life

Did you know that for everything there is a season? A time for every matter under heaven. Ecclesiastes 3:1. This is the time when we see the Clouds cooling temperatures begin to change in the season before you the season know it; it will be spring, and summer again. It is comforting to know, that it is God has set the seasons of life, God has the seasons of the year in place. God has set your life into a different time and season because he has a purpose for you. Each season has a different setting in which we must adjust in our life to grow in Christ. As we discover, and ponder the meaning of each moment, circumstanced season of our lives, we begin to understand our purpose of living. The key is beginning able to enjoy every lesson of each season. If we do not understand; that there is a purpose for every experience, we will not be able to appreciate the beauty of life, we must accept that there are times of weeping, knowing that there is a reason behind every season; and that the next step is to learn something for every season, instead of feeling anxious about the coming season in what God will teach us next. Which season of life are you in right now?

The Strategies of Jesus

Jesus was Spiritually prepared to do the works of and to meet the on-slaughter of the enemy. If we are to be equally prepared to face, and defeat the enemy we must learn, and used the strategies of Jesus used in his life, and ministry. God will gird you with strength unto the battle: Thou hast subdued under you those that rose up against you. Jesus faced Satan knowing He was the son of God. Jesus will give a new commandment into you, that you love one another, as I have love you; that you also love one another. John 8:41-42 Ye do the deed of your father Then said they to him, we be not born fornication; We have one father, even God said Jesus unto them, if God were your father, Ye would love me, for I proceeded forth, and came from God, neither came I of myself; but he sent me. Romans 8:24-25-26 For we are saved by hope, for what a man sees the, why doth he yet hopes for? Verse 25 But if we hope for that we see not, then do we with patience wait for it. Verse 26 Likewise the spirit also helping our infirmities; for we know not what we should pray for as we ought: but the Spirit itself maketh intercession for us with groaning which cannot be uttered.

Why does God collect our tears in a bottle

While in the custody of his enemies, David wrote," You have kept count of my tossing' put my tears in your bottle"(Psalm 56:8. To tell my wanderings: put thou my tears into thy bottle: are they not in thy book? David was going through a difficult time. He begins this sad Psalm with the words' 'Be gracious to me, O God, for man, tramples on me, all day long an attacker oppresses"(Psalm 56:1-2 -3 Be merciful unto me, Oh God: for man would swallow me up; he is fighting daily oppress 2. Mine enemies would daily swallow me up: for they be many that fight against me O thou most high 3. What time Am afraid, I will trust in thee. The Philistines had captured David in Goth-David was at the time he wrote this Psalm, a prisoner of war, and he had reason to cry, and be sorrowful David say that his struggles are recorded in God's Book(verse 8) Thou tell my wanderings: put thou my tears into thy bottle: are they not in thy book? What does this poetic language mean? Does God really write in a Book?

The idea behind the keeping of tears in a bottle" is remembrance. David is expressing a deep trust in God will remember his sorrow and tears and will not forget about him. David is confident that God is on his side. He says, in the midst of this troubling time, This I know God is for me'(Psalm 56:9 When I cry unto Thee, then shall mine enemies turn back: this I know; for God is for me.

God remembers all the things that happen in our lives, including the suffering endured for his sake. In fact, there are many instances in Scripture of God's recondition of man's suffering. God is a tender-heated Father to us, a God who feel with us and weeps with us. Our tears are not futile. God knows each of his children intimately, and every tear we shed has meaning to him.

He remembers our sorrow as if he kept each tear in a bottle. In the end, he will share his joy with us when he wipes every tea from their eyes. There will be no more death or mourning or drying or pain, for the old order of things has passed away"

Tears a Language God-understands

The first time in the Old Testament we see the word tears let's look in 11 King 20:4-5 Isaiah was gone out into the middle court, that the word of the Lord came to him saying, turn again and tell Hezekiah the captain of my people, thus saith the Lord, the God of David your father, I have heard your prayers, I have seen your tears: Behold, I will heal you: on the third day you shall go up unto the house of the Lord.

God has a bottle that catches your tears. God has a book, that tells him about your tears. God is making notes of when you are sad or low in sorrow with grief. Why would God do this for us It goes beyond are comprehension its beyond belief to the nature mind. Sometimes We need to cry! Tears can come in sorrow or sometimes, when we are fearful and feel so helpless, Tears can come easily. Tears are words that our heart can't express. Treas are a language when there are no verbal words.

Our eyes need to be washed by our tears, to soften the ground of are life. God has heard your prayers, and he has seen your tears. God wants to heal your life, for he has written about you, and taken each tear, and collected them in his bottle. How precious is God to take the time and read your tears. Tears and weeping are a form of words that appear 200 times in the Bible, and did you know that tears come from the depths of your soul.

God's Purpose

God doesn't want us to waste our lives away. God wants you to find your purpose in life, and not look at your past, but face the present. Say Yes lord. Then believe it! For God brought you through time and time again. I know in the Spirit he will do it again, for God loves you so much. We come into the New Year! And we reflect on 2019 leaving it behind, and looking onto the New Year, 2020. We need to remember to keep our focus and fix on Christ. No matter what happens in the next year, whether it bring blessing or hard times?

Let's make sure to hold on lean on, trust God more than anything in these trouble times Christian is called to be on guard! Spiritual; standing, strong, foot on the ground firmly. Standing strong in the word of God. Be courage, and to everything in life. Now I would like to share with you about the storms of life.

There are storms in home, marriages, at work and at churches; these are storms which manifest themselves in the secret places of the heart. What you and I need to remember today as we face are own storms. It is because the Lord has sent us into it. Some people have problems with the truth 'But it actually gives our life comport. If just one area of our lives is outside of God's control today, then we are in serious troubles.

I f Satan, the world, or this flesh is able to disrupt are lives apart from the permission of God. Then no area of life.

However: If walking on the water just knowing Jesus will take care of care of you through the storms of this world. Believe God; than whatever it brings into your life. It will work out for are good and his glory. Roman 8:28And we know that all things work together for good to them that love God, to them who are called according to his purpose. Jesus knows how to calm and bridle the storms, which you will be able to face God the end he will come and whisper peace to you in the midst of your trails. God's power is like walking on the water. Just knowing Jesus will take care of you from the storms of this world.

This is his promise. Jesus is coming for the signs in this world are pointing to it. When we are walking with him in faith and using us in a fantastic way in these last days. When we are not walking in faith, he is not able to use in the way he would like to. If you are in a storm today in your life, you need to know; that God can calm your storm. Go to him and he will come and calm your storms in your life, because he loves you very much. He is waiting with his arms open wide for you.

Be careful of your Thoughts

Be careful of your thought's become your words.

Be careful of your words, for your words become your actions.

Be careful of your actions, for your action becomes your habits.

You must be careful of your habit for your habits become your Character. Be careful of your character becomes your destiny.

Let me help you see something! What we think often comes out of our mouth, and into someone else ears. Our words impact how we feel about ourselves and, they can impact how we feel. Words are symbols that communicate what's going on inside our heads to ourselves and to others. We share our fears, our sorrow, our joy, our lives and our dreams with our words.

Our word create action. Our words can create a closeness or a separation with our words we can imitate ourselves to do things we really thought we could do. Our words also move others to step forwards into their own personal power, so they can be of service to their community. Words can calm and words can actually change the direction of a nation.

Also watch what you think and be aware of the words that

comes from your thoughts, and the actions that fellows your words. The enemy doesn't fight you for where you're going. You may be facing difficulty, and it's because God has something amazing in store for you. You're going to see Ephesians 3:20 Now unto him that is able to do exceedingly abundantly above all that we ask or think, according to the power that worth in us. Abundantly above what you could ask, or think can be yours. You and God are a majority, if God be for you who dare be against you. What God has proposed for your life will come to pass, God plans for your life is down to the very second, God he has already considered every attack that will come against you. If it's not your time any enemy, justice or sickness. Isaiah 59:19 The sun shall be no more thy light by day; neither for brightness shall the moon give light unto thee; but the LORD shall be unto thee an everlasting light, and thy God thy glory.

People are watching you

God records our every word and every thought in our daily lives. The precious blood of Christ; as of a lamb without spot. These are the things that shows that we are the possession of our lord ...

People should see Jesus in you. You see! People will look at us and are actions. Remember that you will never know who's watching your actions and what you say. We as Gods children should seek to be led by the Holy Spirit; we must never forget that the Holy Spirit is leading us to righteousness and to being conformed into the Image of Christ, so that our lives will glorify God.

God calls us to live our lives by every word that proceeds from our mouths. You see our lives by every word that process from our moths. You see people who are not believers are living all around us. The word see mean observe; not a pass in glance 'but a concentrated effort, People are making mental notes on us.

People are making mental notes on us. People are watch you to see if we claim to be a true believer. People are watching to see if our behavior matches our belief, if our behavior matches our belief, if we walk matches our talk, and if our character matches our confession, and what we claim to believe.

A person who lives with integrity is whole their lives are put to the test every day in our integrity, and virtually in every situation. We are being watched to see how we respond. Remember we must talk the talk than we must walk the walk of God.

God's Strength

We need to recognize, that all that we are, and all that we will ever be is accomplish through his strength, and not our own.

When we wait on the Lord God, for he is shaping, and preparing us for something so amazing, and so wonderful in our life, that we would not have ever thought of.

God's strength comes from asking him to given you forsaking all things, that would block his presence in your life, for he will wash you as white as snow.

God's Love

God loves you whether you believe it or not. If you can't see it, it's hard for you to grasp something when you haven't learned how to recognize it and experience it. You don't know now to embrace it If you don't know the realization, that God loves you wants you to know about him.

The important thing that God wants you to know is, that his love is awesome, and what he has for you. God wants you to know that he loves you enough to reach across every boundary; that you cannot possibly know.

The boundaries God had to cross to save you, so that you would not go to Hell, whether you believe it or not. God's love is there, and it will always be there. He is just waiting for you and if so, that you can see and understand how much he loves you.

This is amazing love for those who have put their faith and trust in the hands of Jesus. We know that Jesus knows he will never give up on you.

Aging in God

Woman of God! Genuinely believe, that when we live each day for Christ; we will bear the fruit of prosperity good health wholeness and a sound mind, even unto are old age. When we serve God in our lives we will age gracefully, and will grow up into the wisdom, and knowledge that we can share with others.

When we go through the changes in are life's having close walk with a deep relationship with God; we will begin to grow heighten and a deeper width with the joy and strengthen in are bodies. God will put his strength within us, so are bod's will be strong. God's beauty will shine through us.

"Why" because God are Savior knowing every sufficient for are lives, and we can find grace and favor in his sight. We as daughters of God; should walk with our shoulder back; because we are woman and man that lives right in the sight of God. God image of his sons and daughters are well-put together given nails, hair make-up with all who come contact with us will not only be impressed we look, but the glory of God's light flowing through are lives.

Truly People of God will want to spend time in his presence. What I would like you to know; that Love my siblings in Christ and spend fun times of fellowship. I would like to say again, God's grow is sufficient, you can find grace, in his sight. God cause and will not withhold any good thing from the man and woman who seek who walk upright in him.

God's Sovereign Love

I John 4:10 Herein is love, not that we loved God, but that he loved us, and sent his son to be the precipitation for our sins. God pours out his blessing continually on his people. Paul comments on these matters in Ephesus 1:3—5. Grace is God acting freely in his own nature is love; with no promises or obligations to fulfill; in acting of course, righteously –view of the cross. If you put your dreams hopes, in God' then he will take care of your future. Those that have been around a long time can remember singing.

It's so sweet to trust in Jesus or count your blessings name them one by one. The great blessing that God has given to his people is Jesus, in fact it is the greater than any sum of good. Remember David who wrote the book of Psalms, and how he became a powerful King in the land, and was so successful, and was very rich and popular in the land. David knows that in Gods hand that his future was secure, in spite of any problem he might encounter.

Isn't it wonderful to know that Jesus Christ is our redeemer, and Savior are future?

In God's hands to work out his sovereign will in are life. If we love God, he will enable us to see and do his will. In John 14:21 He that hath my commandment, and keepeth them, he it is that love me Father, and I will love him, and will manifest myself to him … If anyone loves me, he will keep my word, and my father will love him, and we will come to him, and make our home with him. The word, the helper, the Holy Spirit whom the father will send in my name, will teach you all things, and bring to your remembrance all things that I said to you.

To know the will of God, we should immerse ourselves in the written word of God, saturating our minds with it, that the result is what is good, acceptable, and the perfect will do God. We should seek to be the Holy Spirit." we must never forget that Holy Spirit is leading us to righteousness and to being conformed into the Image of Christ Jesus so that our lives will glorify God.

God calls us to live our lives by every word that proceeds from our mouths. Did you know that God records our every word and every thought in our daily lives? Job 34:21-23 God watch everything we do. No evil person can hide in the darkness. And so, God does not need to set a time for judgment. As we live with the precious blood of Christ, as the lamb without blemish without spot, these are the things that marks us as Christians that shows that we are the possessions of our Lord. People should see Jesus in you. You see! People will look at our actions in how you treat other people, and how we live. So, remember; that we will leave a legacy for others to see. You will never know who is around listening and watching your actions in what you say and do.

The Breath of God

The Spirit of God spoken to me and gave me a powerful word. The father breath of God is blowing from the four corners of the earth. Do you hear the winds blowing? Do you sense the presence of my Spirit for? Am coming for a people that are looking for me.

I'm coming foe a people who are crying out to me. For I have the antidote to this Virus, that I'm going to destroy, and it will be no more. Hear me well!! what I have spoken I'm shaking this universe in a way it has never known as I did in Pharaohs Day for what I have declared in my word shall come to pass. What I declared in My word shall come to pass.

My Universe I had created you will know that Aim God and I live forever. I had to allow this virus to come for a purpose to wake up my people, ready. I'm about to heal this land and wash this virus away. Get ready; you will see my hand moving like you have never seen before as the days of Pharaoh.

Praise me, worship me, so you can begin to walk into your promise land and thank me for this virus had not have come the Americas would never be the same in what was going happen to it. Cry out to me and know that aim the son of the living God. For blessing and favor is coming to the household of faith in this season, so lock up for my redemption draweth nigh. For the people of this world will know that I'm the God of this universe.

In the palm of God's hand

God has you in his palm of his hand for the future is in unreleased your destiny. Your future is not ahead of you, 'But it's trapped within you. God is more committed to your success than you are. You are not free until your past has no effect on your future. Your destiny is chosen by God. Your future is certain. Whether you arrive there is up to you. I will succeed this year, 'I will'. God places the future of everything. Only those who **"DARE"** fail greatly can ever achieve **"GREAT"** Your destiny requires your cooperation. Your destiny will require making God led choices.

God designed you for your destiny-'In Jeremiah 1;5Before I formed thee in the belly I knew thee; and before thou came forth out of the womb I sanctified Thee, and I ordained thee a prophet unto the nations. Did you know that you were specially designed for your destiny your task was not an afterthought by God—it springs out of our personality, gifts, and the way you are made.

When you are walking in your destiny, it fits like a glove. The desires of the heart reflect God's purpose for your life. Proverbs 37;5 Commit thy way unto the LORD; trust also in him; and he shall bring it to pass. God wants you to delight in your heavenly father and he will give you the desires of your heart. Destiny is something you are, not something you do. When we were born to be and what you have done with your life so far. The more you become who you were made to be, the more you will do what you were born to do.

In Ephesians 1;4 According as he hath chosen us in him before the foundation of the world, that we should be holy and without blame before him in love. Just as he chose us in him before the foundation of the world, he loved having us adoption as sons by Jesus Christ to himself, according to good pleasures of his will. Your whole life prepares you for your destiny.

Every event and circumstance have meaning, because God leverages each experience to help you accomplish his purpose for your life. The refining transforms you into the image of Christ and prepares you to be part of his bride-Romans 8:28. And we know that all things work together for good to them that love God, to them who are called according to his purpose.

Your destiny is bigger than you—Our ultimate fulfillment comes not from pursuing happiness for ourselves, but form bringing life to others for the sake of the kingdom. If your dreams don't involve serving others in a way that stretches you way beyond your limit, then it is not big enough. It really is more blessed to give than to receive. You must die to fulfill your destiny while God's desire is that we live an abundant life, a direct pursuit of happiness can never reach it. True joy only comes through are will with God's purposes.

Only those who lose their life will truly find it. John 12:24 Verily Isay unto you, except a corn of wheat fall into the ground and die, it abides alone: but if it dies, it brings forth much fruit. God has already provided everything you will ever need to successfully to complete your mission. Are you willing to do whatever he asks you to do? Have you made that life changing commitment to trust him with your entire life if you have not yet? Today or tonight would be the best time to make that decision. God has given us a free will we to choose. It is our choice what we are going to do with what we have been freely given. I want you to realize you can be a world changer station. Remember a journey always starts with a first step.

Do you want to make an impact in this world?

Do you want to be a positive influence to others? Your assignment is for a specific group of people.

In fact, they are waiting for you to start your assignment. Their lives may depend on whether you complete it or not. I want you to understand how important your life is to others. There are people that have made a major impact in your life. Whether you realize it or not you have also made an impact in the lives of lives of others of other as well God wants you to dream big. Why? Your destiny is big. He knows you better than you do, and he knows you cannot fulfill your destiny alone. God desire to help you. You will not complete your mission without his assistance. God also has people that will support you and encourage you as you live out your life's mission. Pray that God will put people into your life, so you can live the life you are meant to live.

He wants you to take it with him. God is leading you, but must be willing to do it God's way is the best way; patience will be required to walk on the path he is called you to walk on with him. Understanding that God truly does want you to succeed and prosper. He takes pleasure in the prosperity of his servants. God's way is the only way you will fulfill your destiny the way Good intended it to be completed successfully.

Are you willing to give up your ways?

You may think you know the best way to live your life, but God knows what is truly best for you. God has given you a handbook on how to live this life. He has given you. It is the Bible. It has every answer you will ever need about any area of your life manual and reveal to you how much he loves you, accept you, and desires to be with you in an intimate relationship.

You ask what does that have to do with fulfilling your destiny? It will be out of your personal, and relationship with God that will live out your life the way God created it for his glory. You need to decide when you are going to live your life God's way will it be today or tonight? Other lives are at stake. Take that step and begin to live your life God's way The choice is up to you.

Through the storm

The Eagle is called the king Bird's it said that the Eagle can fly the highest of any bird. The eagles fly streetlight towards the sun, and their wings are used to carry them high into the skies. As Christians we are Heavenly citizens, and we are to lead heavenly lives! How are we to rise unto the heavens unless we have eagle's wings. If God created the eagles with strong wings to be able to raise high into the heavens, then God will give us wings as eagles to rise above the storms of life. As Gods children, we are to live in Gods Heavenly Joy, our hearts.

How do we get the strength of God? How did the eagle get his powerful wings? The eagle got his powerful wings at birth and is born into royalty. Likewise, we are born with spiritual eagle wings with a royal lineage. Many of us fil to realize that we have within us a divine nature in us. The prophet. Isaiah 40:18-29 Tells us; have you never or understood or do not you know that the Lord is the everlasting God, the creator of all the earth no one can measure the depth of his understand and the power.

Those who are tried and worn-out for need to recognize that all that we have been and all that we are and ever will be to be accomplished through God's strength-and not our own. When we wait on the Lord, he will being to shape and preparing us for something amazing in are live waiting on God is not time

Gain, and we never are able to recognize The waiting in our lives as beings something of any positive value, we see it as an inconvenience an interior-eruption I to our activity: The traffic light that holds us up when no one else is coming in the other direction; or the long lines at the grocery or the banks. Most of things that really matter in life, does not happen in a moment it comes for those who have learned to wait on him.

To wait upon the Lord' 'means to let God be God in your whole life. It means to acknowledging Go offers the promise of something "but we need to go to him and be simple recharge. God will exchange your failing strength for his unfailing enemy, so you can walk in your calling that he has for you.

Understanding the seasons of life

For everything there is a season, and a time for every matter under heaven. Ecclesiastes 3:1 This is the time in the full when we see the cloudy days, and cooler temperatures. What a change! The next time you know; it will be spring, and then summer again. It is comforting to know; that it is God who has set the season of life. Fall, winter, spring. and summer. He has set the seasons of the year for its purpose.

God set our lives onto various times in the season because he has a purpose for us. Each season holds a different setting into, which our lives; must find its part and relevance. As we discover, and ponder the meaning of each moment, circumstance, and season if our lives' we begin to understand our purpose of living.

The key is being able to enjoy every lesson no matter 'what season you are in. If we do not understand that there is a purpose for every experience, we will not be able to appreciate the beauty of life. As we go through our different seasons in our lives. God works in all seasons of life to help us find faith, and grow, and mature in him. God uses every season to teach us something about himself, like faithfulness, his strength, and his power. God can teach you something through your experiences in your season.

Daniel 2:21 say and he changed the times and the seasons; he removes kings and set up kings; he gives wisdom unto the wise, and knowledge to them that know understanding: God tells us that God controls the times of that if sunshine would shine all the time; that it will create a desert, and the soil would turn to sand. God knows how much we need in our life. There are times for us to speak up, and a time to be silent.

God joints your life together with a man, and woman so that God brings out your gifts man abilities can be used for the glory of God. We must accept that there are times of rejoicing as well as time of weeping knowing there is a season behind every season; and that the next is to learn something from every season, instead of feeling anxious about the coming season of life that you are right now.

He told them that you cannot judge a tree, or a person, by only one season. The essence of what they bare is the pleasure, of joy and love that comes from that life can only be measured at the end where all the seasons are up. If you give up when it is winter, the beauty of you walking in summer fulfillment of your fall, and you will miss the promise of your Spring.

Growing Gracefully

Am getting older and I will be 69 this year. It's all happening to all of us, for time seams to slip by. I can remember wanting to be older, so I could drive a car sense that day the time in my life has gone by so fast.

I can remember in my late 20s I wake up and got on my knees praying and asking the Lord Jesus to pour upon me the same anointing that Sara had. In the bible it said that Sara was admire by many kings; for her youthfulness at the age of 90 years old. God poured his anointing on Sara that kept her beautiful as God 's showcases for all to see.

I ask Jesus to pour that same anointing on this child The Holy Spirit ask me, why! that this child would be a showcase to glorify her father in heaven to enhance the kingdom of God, to show woman that they two can have the same anointing that Sara of old had.

All we must do is just ask, as you live your life doing the call of God. As I gotten older in my; late 50s and 60s people would say to my husband Mark does not you think your rocking the cradle; Mark would laugh than I spoke up and said my husband is only 7 months older than me. Then they would look at me and say, you look no older than in your late 40s. When you live your life for Jesus, he will keep his daughters young.

How to age Gracefully

1. see yourself as Jesus sees you
2. Live sacred-Chase God's big dream for you
3. Find someone younger to mentor them
4. Encourage the woman who reminds you of yourself.
5. Embrace your appearance as it changes

We are beautiful inside and out. When we acknowledge Christ's deep and abiding love for us. Pure love that does not change with our accomplishment or appearance. It is always there accepting us exactly for who we are. This prepares and empowers us to go forward and fulfill his will in our destiny.

Over Coming Doubts

Did you know that the number one cause of doubt is thought'
'But not everyone gets healed, so it must not be God's will, do I
probably won't get healing either' 'This thought destroys faith,
is not of God, and it blocks healing? Reject those thoughts.

Do you know that God gives us? Angelic help! As mentioned,
God's perform his word, obeying the voice of his word. JV-
Psalm 103:20. When we speak God's word in faith according
to his will. God will dispatch his angel to make it happen,
bringing it into being' Hold on to God's word. Your healing
will be manifest in you. For his stripes, you have been healed.

'Let me share this with you. If your healing is gradual hold
on, please do not give up on faith because when you give up on
your faith it canceled your healing. I tell you your healing will
come in his perfect timing. Again—do not ever give up! Never
say oh well it's not working. 'Which will cancel your healing.

Awesome God

God loves you whether you believe it or not. If you cannot see it; it is hard for you to gasp something when you have not learned how to recognize it and experience it. You do not know now to embrace it. If you do not know the realization, that God loves you and wants you to know about him.

The important thing that God wants you to know is that his love is awesome and what he has for you. God wants you to know that he loves you enough to reach across every boundary; that you cannot know.

The boundaries God had to cross to save you, so that you would not go to hell, whether you believe it or not. God's love is there, and it will always be there. He is just waiting for you and if so; that you can see and understanding how much he loves you. This is amazing love for those who have put their faith and trust in the hands of Jesus

People Change

No matter how good a person is, sometimes they can hurt you because of this; we must forgive. It takes years to build trust and only seconds to destroy it … We do not have to the change friends if we understand that friends change …

The circumstances and the environment influence our lives, but we are the ones, who are responsible for ourselves. that you must control you and your actions, or they will control you. that patience requires much practice that there are people who love us, but simply do not know how to show it that sometimes the person you think will hurt you and make you fall is instead one of the few who will help you get up …

You should never tell a child that dreams are fake, it would be a tragedy if they knew. It is not always enough to be forgiven by someone in most cases you must forgive yourself first. That no matter in how many pieces your heart is broken … The world does not stop to fix it God wants us to meet all the wrong people first before meeting the right ones so when we finally meet the right one,

The angel from above

I was getting ready for bed when a friend called me, and we began to talk about what God was doing in these last days. At that moment, I told my friend that I began to sense the Holy Spirit coming upon me. I told him I was seeing an angel about 5 ft 6 on the left corner of my room with his hands open wide to me. I looked to my right, and I saw a angel about 11ft tall angel. I knew it was Micheal the angel.

This angel was huge" Micheal stood with a huge sword pointing to the heaven's Than suddenly the Micheal slowly put down the sword by his right side and was smiling at me. I hang up the phone. I went to the bathroom, then began to head back to my bedroom, suddenly Michael stood right in front of me.

The power of God Was so strong I fell on my knees. Michael places the sword on my left shoulder, then he put the sword on my right shoulder, then lay the sword upon my head. At that moment, I felt heaven coming upon me with such glory; glory, like I never felt before. The Lord said to me. This night my daughter I christen you as my Queen for I am pleased with thee.

Faith in Action

How strong is your faith? If you had to rate your faith on a scale from one to ten, where would your faith fall into. Real faith's not demonstrated in confines of Sunday morning worship.

It is revealed in the challenging times of life. Faith is defined in our lives, when we are facing the challenging decisions, and fiery trails of life. Faith in action will be lived out in some practical ways.

Faith

The higher thoughts of Jesus the Greater his power over your soul, and your life in what you will be in him. It means: The deeper you go in God, the more times you spend with him the Word! In intercession in prayer and fasting this means that you will decrease 'but Jesus will increase

We must Remove Our Mask

God what is you to know you are a daughter of the highest. A Holy Princess, a woman with ... of who we are as daughters of the King. As we face are present world. My sister's we as God's children have suffered through the years with insecurity, and betrayal because of this, they have fallen in the trap of pretending to be someone they were never created or called to be.

It's as though they are hiding behind a mask. Without a true understanding of who we are as God's children of the king, as we face the present world, we may not be who we really are underneath. If we are to be God's warriors, that we were meant to be. We must remove the mask; that they are hiding. Did you know that every child passionately in love with Jesus is so priceless, and a warrior?

God always purification process from one sage of our lives to the next. God purifies us through hid word, trails, and tests. God wants to see if we are ready to stand the process. It is during this process; that we ask the question, who am I here for? You see the enemy wants you to stop from fulfilling your destiny and does not want you to realize your full potential or the gifts, and talents, that God has a place inside you, because he knows if you find out he will not be able to stop you. I know there are times in all our lives, that we say, I am ready to get to the next phase of my life.

God is saying we have gone through time seems never easy, because we are always the process, after we've prepared to meet him, we will have the kings favor and his ears, and we will ask what will, and it shall be done for us. God place for our lives takes much preparation time seems never easy, because we're in a hurry trying to get to the end results.

Every one of us must go through a myrrh anointing, that is the season in are life's that is sometimes bitter and painful. God is so concerned with how we go through the process, as he is with the product at the end. God desires, and requires, us to go through his refining, and preparation time, that we may be well- equipped enabled, and capable of fulfilling the task, and purpose for which we were created.

It's the very things that lays the foundation for the time when God displays us as his beautiful princesses. We are the soul fragrance to God's nostrils, as we worship and praise our Lord and King. In scriptural it tells us that are prays are as sweet fragrance, and as we transformed by the presence of are king. This preparation time empowers us to go forward and fulfil his will in our destiny.

Do you have a Goliath in your life

We are like David who stood before his Goliath in our lives, that we face every day. David already put on the shield of God upon him and went and stood before the giant. As the enemy comes like a roar lion to defeat you; that way we must put on the whole armor of God upon you. When the Goliath that is in your life begins to shout at you tells you that you do not have what it takes to be what God call you become, that you do not have the know-how, and the strength to walk through and Win 1, The Goliath in your life begins to wear you down through people to give up, but God wants you to know, that you will make it through.

As God's children you say, I come against Goliath in my life in the mighty name of Jesus for God's shield is upon me. The Lord God, which lives within me will deliver me out of my battle. We have been chosen to walk into are promise land according to the plan of God, who works out everything with purpose of his will into our lives that have been in order, that we who have hope in Christ, might praise him, that we were marked in God with a promise of the redemption of those who are possession to the praise of God glory.

That the same mighty strength when he raised Christ from the dead, and sent Jesus at the right hand in the heavenly realm, because of God's great love for us, God who is rich in mercy and grace made us alive with Christ; even when we were dead in are transgression, it is by grace we have been saved through faith and this is not from ourselves, it is the gift of God---not by works 'that no one can boast. We are called in the riches of Gods glorious inheritance in his faithfulness, so that you may know the Spirit of God better.

I pray that you, may be enlightened in order that you may know the hope to which he has called you for, Gods glorious inheritance in his faithfulness to those who believe. For we are God's handiwork created in Christ Jesus to do good works, which God prepared in advance for us to do' 'But to each one of us Grace has given to us as through Christ Jesus. God teachers us not to judge a man by his height or the way they look like. God choses a man inside, which is a warrior with the power of God, that listen to the voice of God within your Spirit.

Giving trust in God's Provision

The biggest deterrent to giving, is fear. Fear would say' you will give too much, and you won't have enough for other things. We as God children should give above and beyond what is comfortable, and easy by expressing our faith, and truth in God to provide for our family.

Many Christians have discovered the joy of casting their crumbs of bread upon the waters. It is such a joy to see God fulfill his promise of provision when we obey him. It is such a joy to see our father God's smile to become wider. Do you know that Jesus loves a cheerful giver?

Jesus is delighted to see his people gladly opening their hearts and provide for those that are in need in their lives for that opens the door for God to bless you more in our life for you as a Christian makes you happier knowing, that we made Jesus happy, because we have learned that it is better to give than to receive. We must understand; when you bless people when you know that they are in need that moves the heart of God to bless you.

Your Child

Father God! I come to you as your child. Asking for you to fill this child; up completely with your anointing oil to pour upon your child from the top of my head to every part of my body so as this child goes along my way, let my life send the glow of your light of glory Father; let thy oil that is all around me heal, every heart, bondage in people lives. Father just with one touch from your oil and wine will bring healing of divine two every wounded soul. Let it flow and set your people free. Let the bondage and chains drop to the ground setting them free. As your child, walking on the path that you have put this child on, let this child life shine for the glory of God. Thank you, father, for your mercy and grace you have place on my life. Thank you for showing me the way it and setting me free through your blood that was shed on calvary Amen.

Conclusion

God is calling you to the throne room as his princess and prince; Warriors where he is inviting you to come into his presence, so he can love you. Your King and your father desires to teach you who you really are in Christ Jesus as you pick up your sword, the word of God, and are ready to believe it and be transformed by it!

So, daughters and sons of God rise, for the king God is calling you to battle. He wants you to move forward and recognize the incredible woman and men you are and see what you are becoming as who he created you to be. The enemy would love nothing more than to convince you that predation and the time is too long, and you're not prince or princess material, but it is not time, God already sees the prince/ princess of you, and you have come to the kingdom for such a time as this.

My Lover My Savior

You are my redeemer, my friend forever
that's what you are. You raise me up to face another day
You are the peace that I love, for with every passing
second, you are the strength, that fills my soul,
and lets me press on for you are the love that
I cannot get enough of you. For you are my savior

Greatest Gift

The greatest gift that a mother, Grandma
could ever give to her
Daughter, Son, Granddaughter is to
share what my grandma taught
Me. When you go on your own; remember
in life, you will always
reap what you sow kindness Grace,
Mercy. Words are like fresh
water that sparkles with love. When
you reach out to people with
love to a friend, that same hand one
day might life you up. You
will see what goes around, will always
come back to you. Its is so
important, that you put these keys into your life

Let me rest in you

Let me rest in your heart
Let me sense your embrace
For you are my sunshine
fill my life with you close
to my heart Never let me go
Hide me under your wing
So warm and complete

My wonderful wife

When I first met you, though you were a young teenager
The stars in your eyes, with your warm personality.
Draws me to you I love the way you love people, and your
family Because you are a Christian, and had a deep
relationship with God I grew to love you more with a deep
love each day in our relationship. Today
After 50 years of Marriage.
I love the way you worship in the spirit We always
forgive, and make up before the end
of day. Our love was knitted
together by God, and the ultimate thing
I enjoy about you, when we
minister together.

Jesus Valentine's Day

Jesus does not send perfume to linger in the air
Instead, he sends salvation, sweet to show how much he cares.
He does not bring me candy hearts in boxes of delight
Instead, he always lets me know I'm precious in his sight.
He does not send out pretty cards trimmed in shades of red
Instead, he gave his life for me. His precious blood was shed.
He does not hand out fancy gifts like
we would send to our mother.
Instead, he sends a message clear to always love each other.

God's Love

Now I know what love is. Love is the touch of your
hand, when I become frightened.
Love is the warmth of your embrace when I'm lonely
Love is the joy we sense, whatever I know you are near
Love is the excitement that fills my soul,
when you talk with me
Love is when you hold me and feel complete
Love knows you will always be there to pick me up.
Love knows you will always be there, and you will never
leave me or forsake me Jesus stir in me a passion
stronger than human desire.
Jesus stirs in a passion pure and all-consuming Holy fire,
so, this child can pour it upon your people.

Facing Struggles

When we face struggles, we often wonder why?
Years from now, Though we may realize, that it
were those struggles, that taught us something
We could not have otherwise learned
that there was a purpose in our pain
God's purposes are greater than your pain, and he has a
greater purpose than you will ever know
Help me to hold on firmly to the promise in keeping
my eyes only on you and peace will overtake you in
your life for God will complete what
he sets out to do in your life

Printed in the United States
by Baker & Taylor Publisher Services